Play With Plants

PLAY
WITH
PLANTS

NEWLY REVISED EDITION

Millicent E. Selsam
photographs by Jerome Wexler

WILLIAM MORROW AND COMPANY
New York 1978

Library of Congress Cataloging in Publication Data

Selsam, Millicent Ellis (date)
  Play with plants.

  Summary: Directions for growing plants from the roots, stems, leaves, or seeds of common potatoes, beans, and house plants. Tells how a seed grows and presents simple gardening experiments.
  1. Botany—Experiments—Juvenile literature. 2. Indoor gardening—Juvenile literature. [1. Botany—Experiments. 2. Experiments. 3. Indoor gardening. 4. Gardening] I. Wexler, Jerome. II. Title.
QK52.6.S44 1978   635   78-8509
ISBN 0-688-22166-1
ISBN 0-688-32166-6 lib. bdg.

Printed in the United States of America.
First Edition
1   2   3   4   5   6   7   8   9   10

Acknowledgment for Photographs:

Page 52: Harold Krieger

Pages 54, 58 right, 61, 85: Hart Peterson

Pages 50, 51, 53, 57, 68, 78: Millicent E. Selsam

To Gayle and Stephie

Contents

1

A Typical Plant

Plants can be fun. In this book you will find many different ways of having fun with plants, and all of them depend on growing things in your home. You can grow all the plants in this book without any garden out-of-doors.

First look at a plant. The typical plant has roots, stems, and leaves. The roots hold the plant in place, and they take in water and dissolved minerals from the soil. The stem carries the water and minerals through

special long woody vessels up to the leaves. The leaves manufacture food for the entire plant. The raw materials that they use are water from the soil and carbon dioxide from the air. The air passes into the leaf through pores on the underside of the leaf. Light supplies the energy that combines the carbon dioxide and water into simple sugars. These sugars travel down through other special tubes in the stem and supply energy to all parts of the plant.

But sugar alone is not enough food for the plant. It also needs proteins to manufacture cell walls, protoplasm, and other plant parts in order to grow. To make proteins, the plant uses the minerals dissolved in the water of the soil.

The needs of plants are simple. They require water, light, minerals, and air.

2
Plants Need Water

If you forget to water a plant for a while, it will quickly droop and wilt. A plant cannot live without water.

Too much water can kill a plant too. Roots need air in order to grow, and too much water can fill up all the air spaces in the soil. For this reason, plants are kept in pots just big enough to let them grow. If pots are too big, they hold more water than the roots can take up, and air cannot get to the roots.

Flowerpots usually have holes in the bottom, so that

extra water can run out of them. Some plants are grown in jars or containers without holes, but in these cases pebbles or stones are put underneath the soil to catch extra water.

How do you know when to water? Wait until the surface of the soil *feels* dry before you water. Then do so thoroughly. Keep adding water until it comes out of the bottom of the pot. Then you know all the soil in the pot is wet. Discard this extra water. For most plants grown indoors, use water that has been mixed from the cold and hot water taps until it feels slightly warm.

After you have watered plants a few times, you may begin to wonder how the water gets into the plant from the soil. The part of the plant that is underground is the root, so somehow the water must get into the root.

Most roots have root hairs—tiny, delicate, little hairs that extend from the surface of the root into the soil. Their walls are so very thin that water and minerals can easily pass through them into the center of the root.

To get a good look at root hairs, try this experiment. Soak a clean small flowerpot in water for an hour. Then place it upside down in water. Stick *soaked* radish seeds onto the outside of the wet flowerpot. It's tricky, but with a little practice you can get the radish seeds to stay on. Now cover the whole thing with a cooking pot to keep the flowerpot moist and dark. Roots grow better in the dark. The photographs show the way the radish seeds look after two days.

16

ROOT
HAIRS

The water that gets into the root through the root hairs travels up through the root into the stem.

Since a carrot is a root, a big one, let's see how it carries water up to the stem.

First cut the carrot straight down through the middle. You can see that the carrot has a central core. In this center are tubes that carry water up from the soil to the stem. If you cut a thin slice across the carrot and hold it up to the light, you will see this central core clearly.

Now prove to yourself that the carrot supplies water to its stems and leaves. Get a young carrot with fresh stems and leaves and freshen them up still more by cutting off the bottom tip of the root and putting the carrot in a glass of water. If you cannot find carrots with stems and leaves attached, take one from a package sold in the supermarket and keep it in water till new leaves form.

Color some water with green or red ink. Use two droppersful of ink to a half glass of water.

Now put the carrot into the colored water, and set it in a bright light for several hours. Cut across the middle of the carrot, and notice where the colored ink is. It is all in the tubes in the center.

From the root of the plant, water travels up through the stem into the leaves. You can watch this happen in a stalk of celery. Freshen up a stalk of celery by cutting off the bottom half inch and setting the stalk in water for about an hour. Then put the stalk of celery in water colored by red ink, just as you did for the carrot. Set it in bright light.

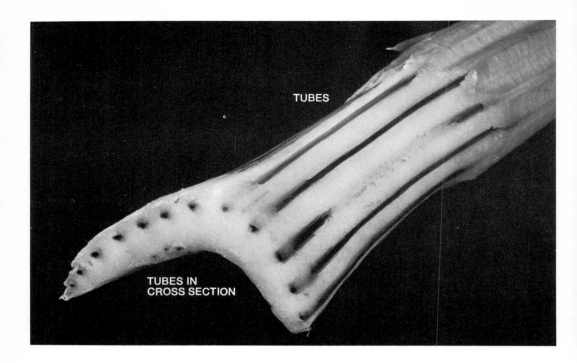

TUBES

TUBES IN
CROSS SECTION

In about an hour, look to see if the leaves of the celery have turned reddish. When they have, you can take the celery out and examine it. First cut off a piece about an inch from the bottom. Look for the red ink.

Now take the rest of the stalk, and with a small knife scrape off the outer layers until you come to red lines. These red lines are tubes that carry water up through the stalk to the leaves.

You probably have seen green carnations on Saint Patrick's Day. These carnations were colored green in the same way that the leaves of the celery were colored red. You can color a white carnation yourself. First cut off the end of the stem under water. In this way you prevent air from blocking the tubes through which the water passes up the stem. Then place the carnation in

20

water colored with red, green, or purple ink, and put it in bright light for a few hours. The petals will become reddish, greenish, or purplish, depending on the color ink you used.

If you want to have fun, try splitting the stem of a carnation into two parts without tearing them from the flower. Put each part into a differently colored

liquid. Keep the flower in bright light for a few hours. The petals will become colored with the color of the liquid that reaches them, and you will have a carnation part of which is one color and part another.

If water is constantly passing from the ground into the roots of a plant and up to the stem and leaves and flowers, it must leave the plant somehow. It does so by evaporating from the surface of the leaves.

You can see for yourself that water leaves the plant. Take a plant growing in a small flowerpot, and water it

well. Put the pot in a plastic bag, and tie the bag snugly around the stem of the plant. The soil and water from the pot are inside the bag, and the plant is outside. Now set a large glass or plastic jar over the pot. Put it in a bright light. If water evaporates from the leaves, it will collect on the glass.

3

Plants Need Light

What a plant looks like depends very much on how much light it gets. Try growing the same kind of plant in very bright light, in dim light, and in the dark. You will be amazed at how different it can look.

Soak twelve pea seeds overnight. (You can use the dry peas you buy in a package in the supermarket or grocery.) Plant four peas in each of three flowerpots. Water the soil, and slip plastic bags over the pots to prevent drying.

Now put one pot in very bright light (sunlight if possible), one in medium light, and one in the dark (covered with a pot or in a dark closet).

After a week, compare the looks of your plants. The picture shows three pea plants—one grown in the dark, one in medium light, and one in bright light. You can see how important light is to the growth of the plant. If a plant is not getting enough light, it is tall, leggy, and pale, while plants grown in good light are green and stocky. So if you have a sunny windowsill, use it. Even bright light rather than direct sunlight will help your plant.

Of course, some plants need less light than others. They are usually the ones grown for their leaves alone and not for their flowers.

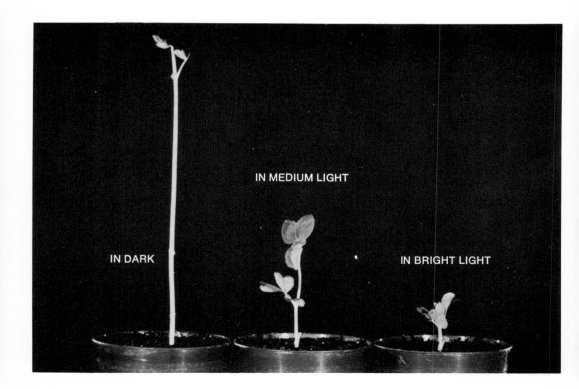

IN MEDIUM LIGHT

IN DARK

IN BRIGHT LIGHT

Have you ever seen a lopsided plant with the leaves all turned in one direction? It is easy to change a lopsided plant into a straight one. All you have to do is to turn the plant around so that the other side will get light. If you never turn your plants, their leaves will face out and you will miss much of their beauty.

Leaves and young stems always bend toward the light.

Did you notice how much the bean plants placed on the windowsill turned toward the light?

Sunlight is made up of lots of colors. If you have ever looked at a rainbow, you have seen them. Which colors does the plant use—red, blue, yellow, green? Experiments have shown that a plant mostly uses the red and blue rays in the food-making process.

Since fluorescent lights have these rays, you can use this artificial light to grow plants. Many people now grow plants in dark corners, bookshelves, or on plant stands where fluorescent lamps can be mounted in a

fixture over the growing area. It is a good idea to mix several kinds of fluorescent tubes, such as daylight, cool white, and warm white tubes, because they differ in the amount of blue and red light they give off.

4
Potting

Containers

A container for growing plants can be anything from a plastic glass to a flowerpot. Look around your kitchen for plastic containers used to store food in the refrigerator and for plastic cottage-cheese containers. You might even use a plastic bread box or plastic-coated paper cups. Aluminum-foil cake pans make good plant containers too.

Whatever you use, there must be holes in the bottom

so that extra water can run out. Punching them in paper cups and aluminum-foil pans is easy. But to make holes in hard plastic containers you have to heat a skewer or ice pick in a gas flame or on the heating coil of an electric stove. When it is hot, push it through the bottom of the plastic container. The skewer stays hot enough to make several holes at one time.

If you have never planted seeds before, try the new Jiffy pellets or One-steps, which can be bought in any garden-supply place or florist shop. When dry, they are flat, thin discs. Put them in a quarter cup of water, and in about ten minutes they change into tiny flowerpots. The pellets are made of sterile peat moss and soak up water quickly.

JIFFY PELLETS

DRY   WET

To plant tiny seeds, just press them into the peat moss. To plant larger seeds, take out enough of the peat so that you can insert the seed and cover it.

Keep the pellets in a container to which you can add water. They won't need water until the seeds sprout if you slip a plastic bag over the container. When the plants push through the soil, remove the plastic bag and put the container in a brightly lighted or sunny place. After the plastic bag is removed, you must be sure to add water to prevent the Jiffy pellets from drying out.

The pellets are easy to use, and because they are made of sterile peat moss, they prevent seedlings from toppling over from a fungus disease called "damping-off."

Soil

If you cannot get Jiffy pellets, you can plant seeds in any plastic container or flowerpot that you fill with soil. The best kind to use is the ready-mixed sterilized potting soil you can buy in any five-and-ten or at a florist shop. (Ordinary garden soil is too full of weeds and pests.) To make sure the potting soil is loose enough, you can use one third sterile soil, one third vermiculite, and one third perlite. Vermiculite looks like a pearly cereal, and perlite looks like coarse white sand. Both can be bought in the five-and-ten. They tend to keep the soil from packing down, and they allow water to run through freely, so air reaches the roots.

Put the soil in the container to within an inch of the

PERLITE

VERMICULITE

top. Scatter the seeds on the surface, and cover them with soil. If the seeds are tiny, just cover lightly. If the seeds are thick, cover with twice as much soil as the seed is thick. Slip a plastic bag over the container, and keep it in a warm place. Check to make sure the soil stays damp. When the plants are two inches high, remove the bag and put the container in a brightly lighted place. Remember to water.

Moving Plants to Bigger Pots

When the roots of the plants begin to fill the pellet, and the plants are two to three inches high, transfer the pellet to a bigger pot. Doing so is easy on the plant, because the roots are not disturbed.

34

READY TO BE
TRANSPLANTED

Use a four-inch flowerpot or container. If you are using a clay flowerpot with a big hole in the center, put a few pieces of broken pottery over the hole. If you are using a plastic pot with a small hole, you don't need the crockery.

Fill the pot or container one third full with sterile soil (see page 33), place the pellet on the soil, fill in around it, and cover it with more soil.

If you are not using pellets and have many seeds growing in a container, you have to lift each seedling out separately and move it to a separate pot. To do so, gently loosen the soil underneath a seedling with a pencil or stick and lift the plant out by the leaves. Fill a four-inch pot with soil. Then use the pencil to make a hole deep enough to receive the roots. Place the plant in the hole, tamp down around it, water it, and keep it in a dimly lighted place for a few days. Then transfer the plant to a sunny windowsill.

If you want to keep only one plant, save the best seedling and pull out all the others.

The time will come when a plant has to be moved from a small pot to a larger one, because the plant roots have entirely filled the pot. To do so, water the plant first. Then hold the stem between your fingers and rap the rim of the pot against a hard surface. In this way

you loosen the ball of earth in the pot so that it slides out in one whole piece. Take a pot about one inch larger than the old one. Put a few pieces of broken pottery over the hole (if it is a big one), and add about an inch of fresh sterile soil. Put the plant on it, add more soil, then tamp the soil down around the plant.

After a plant has been growing in a pot for several months, the minerals in the soil will be exhausted. At this point you have to use a fertilizer. The liquid fertilizers that you can find in the five-and-ten or any florist shop are easiest to work with. But fertilizer powders and pellets are available also.

Plants that are growing actively should be fertilized every two weeks.

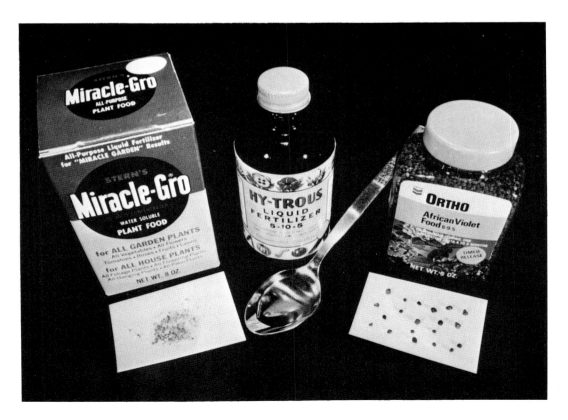

5

Plants Grow from Seeds

Seeds are wonderful things. They look dry and dead, but if you give them water and warmth, they will come to life. Inside every seed there is the beginning of a new plant. Let's look into a seed and find it.

We'll choose a big one to work on, so that the parts will be easy to see. Soak some lima-bean seeds overnight so that they will swell and be full of water. Look for the scar on the side of the bean. The scar shows where the seed was attached to the inside of the bean pod. Now

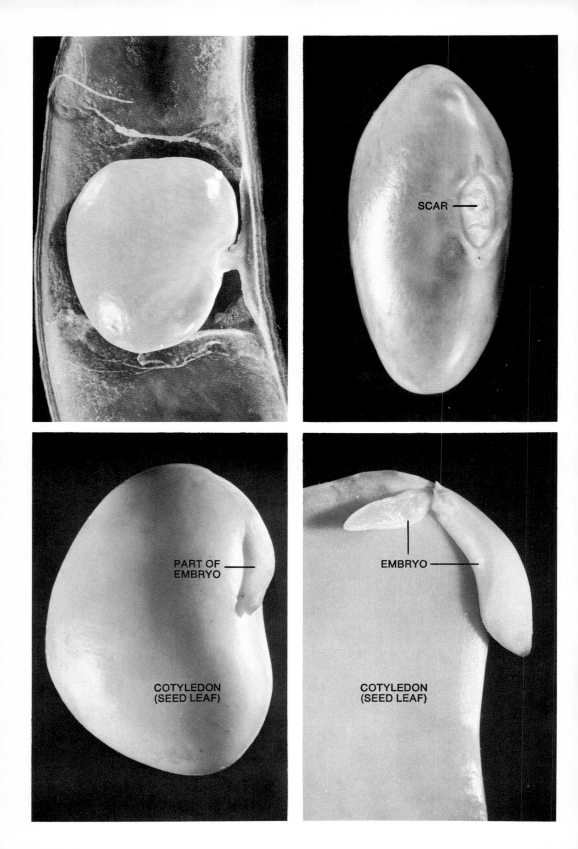

SCAR

PART OF EMBRYO

COTYLEDON (SEED LEAF)

EMBRYO

COTYLEDON (SEED LEAF)

take off the seed coats. They should slip off easily when the seed is wet. What you have left can be split into two parts. Do so carefully and gently. These two parts are called seed leaves, or cotyledons (kah-till-*ee*-duns). They have lots of food stored in them. Attached to them you can see a very tiny baby plant. It is called an "embryo."

Look at this embryo carefully. Use a magnifying glass if you can. Roots will grow out from the bottom of the embryo. Stem and leaves will grow from the top. The mystery of the seed is solved. Inside a seed there is an embryo and some food to start off its life. All it needs is water, warmth, and air in order to grow. Then it can become a little plant or a tall tree, depending on what kind of seed it is.

A new young plant cannot grow well without using the food stored in the seed leaves of the seed. Proving so is an interesting experiment.

Soak three dried lima-bean seeds overnight. Line a glass with wet paper towel, and keep water in the bottom of the glass. Now place one whole seed between the paper and the glass. Carefully remove one of the seed leaves from the second bean seed without injuring the embryo. Then place the seed leaf containing the embryo between the paper and the glass. Cut the seed leaves of the third bean seed so that only half of one seed leaf will remain with the baby plant. Place it, too, between the glass and the paper.

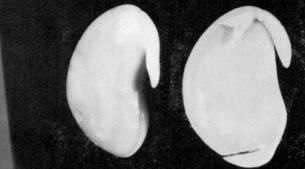

ONE SEED LEAF   WHOLE SEED WITH TWO SEED LEAVES   HALF OF SEED LEAF

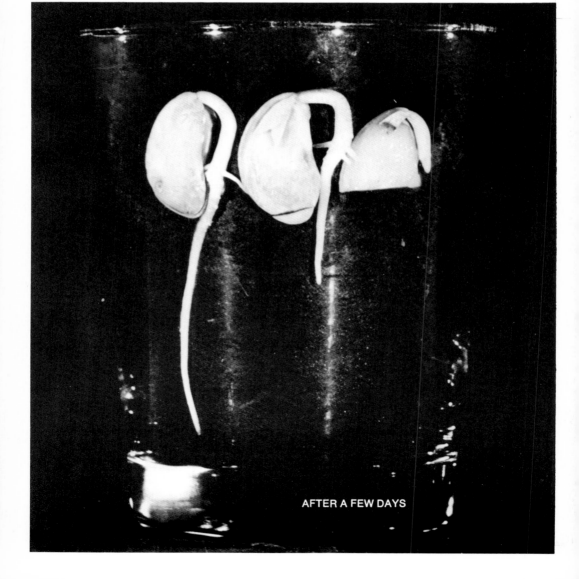

AFTER A FEW DAYS

Now you have three bean seeds ready to grow. The first has both seed leaves. The second has only one seed leaf. The third has half of one seed leaf.

Watch them. You will soon see that the biggest plant grows from the first bean seed. The reason is that this baby plant has the most food. By the time all the food in the seed leaves is used up by the growing plant, it has its own leaves, which can make new food for it.

Starch is one of the foods in the seed leaves. It can also be found in many of the foods we eat. It makes up most of the food in potatoes and rice, for example. You can try this simple way of testing for starch. Make a weak iodine solution by putting a medicine dropperful of iodine into half a glass of water. Drop the iodine solution with a dropper onto a slice of bread or a few grains of rice or a slice of potato. If the food you are testing turns dark blue, you have proved that starch is present.

Now try the iodine solution on a thin slice of *soaked* bean seed. Then you can see the proof of the statement that beans have starch in their seed leaves.

We wait till the ground has warmed up to plant most seeds for a very good reason. Seeds need warmth in order to grow. Try this experiment to prove it.

Soak thirty radish seeds overnight. Lay fifteen of them down on wet paper towels in a dish. Cover them and put the dish in the refrigerator. Do the same thing with the other fifteen seeds, but keep the dish at room temperature instead of putting it in the refrigerator. After

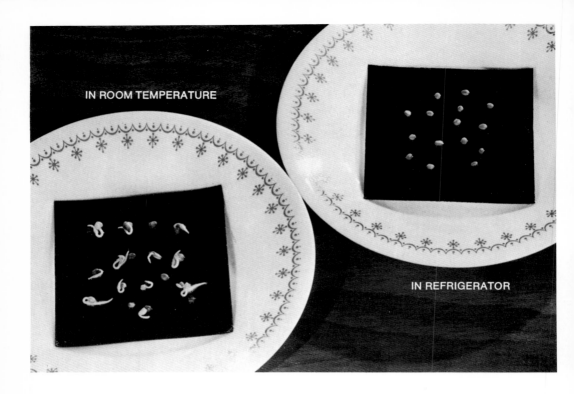

IN ROOM TEMPERATURE

IN REFRIGERATOR

two days, count and note down the number of sprouting seeds in each dish. How many were in the refrigerator, and how many were outside in room temperature? You will have proof then that seeds need warmth to grow.

Besides water and warmth, seeds need air in order to start growth. Here is another experiment to test this statement.

Collect three small glass jars of the same size. Baby-food jars or any other small jars will do. Fill one jar with water from the faucet. This water has air dissolved in it. Add fifteen radish seeds. Fill the second jar with water boiled, to drive out all the air, and then cooled. Add fifteen radish seeds. Fill the third jar also with boiled and cooled water. Add fifteen radish seeds. However, seal

46

WATER FROM FAUCET

BOILED WATER WITH PARAFFIN SEAL

BOILED WATER

this jar by pouring melted paraffin over the surface of the water.

All three jars contain the same number of seeds—fifteen in each one. After two days, count the number of seeds in each jar that have started to grow. Keep a careful record of the results of your experiment.

You do not have to buy packages of seeds to plant, for there are many seeds that come into your kitchen as food. Some come in packages that you find on the grocery shelf. Many come from the vegetables and fruits you buy to eat.

Scientifically speaking, a fruit is the part of a plant that has seeds in it. So a lot of things called vegetables are really fruits. It is hard to think of a green pea pod

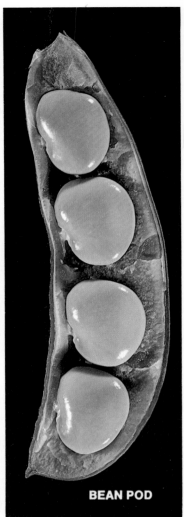

SQUASH　　　　**BEAN POD**

or a string bean as a fruit. But they have seeds in them, and so a scientist would call them fruits. The same is true of a tomato, a cucumber, and a squash. You can easily find the seeds in all of these vegetables and plant them.

When you plant any of these seeds, follow the directions on pages 32-34.

48

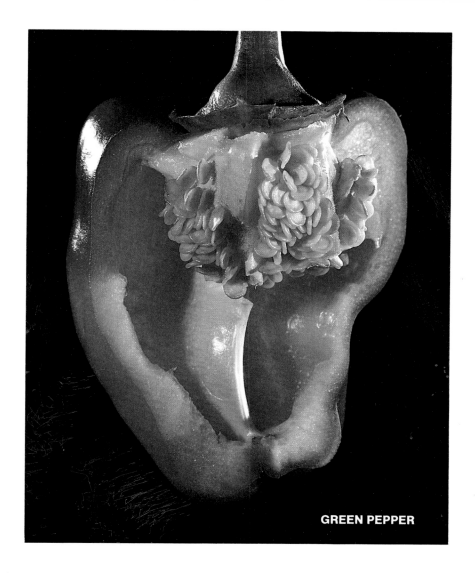

GREEN PEPPER

Beans are easy to grow. You can use kidney beans, lima beans, string beans, pinto beans, black beans, or navy beans. Use the beans from the packages you buy in the supermarket or grocery. Or you can plant the fresh beans you take out of a bean pod. The dry beans should be washed and soaked overnight. The fresh beans can be planted without soaking. The different

BEAN PLANT

kinds of bean plants look very much alike except that some are tall climbers and others are short and bushy.

If you live where you can find tiny Chinese mung beans, soak them overnight and plant. They sprout in a few days, and in a week or two you will have lovely plants.

Peas grow into interesting plants too. Plant fresh peas from a pea pod or use the dry peas on the grocery shelf. They, like dry beans, have to be soaked overnight.

Try corn also. The most available seeds are popcorn seeds that you can find in cans all year round. In the summertime, of course, you can take the seeds from an ear of corn. Cut off a piece from the ear of corn, and let it dry for a few days. Then pick off the dry kernels and plant them. In about two weeks the plants will begin to sprout.

PEA PLANT

LENTIL PLANT

Dry lentil seeds from a box grow into delicate plants. Soak them before planting.

Squash seeds are a lot of fun to plant, because you can get flowers within six weeks. Plant one squash seed (taken from a squash "fruit") per pellet. Transfer the plant to a flowerpot when the roots fill the pellet. Then put the pot in a bright, sunny place and keep the soil moist. Add liquid fertilizer every week. The seeds sprout in one week. The plant is a vine with large heart-shaped leaves and surprisingly large yellow flowers.

Watermelon, cantaloupe, and cucumber seeds can be planted in the same way. They too are vines with large leaves and huge yellow flowers.

SQUASH PLANT

GRAPEFRUIT PLANT

The next time you have an orange or grapefruit or lemon in the house, take the seeds out and plant them. Do not allow the seeds to dry out. If necessary, soak the seeds in water until you are ready to plant. The plants have dark-green, glossy leaves and make pretty houseplants.

PEANUT PLANT

The peanut sprouts easily and grows into a lovely plant. The trick is to find fresh, *unroasted* peanuts. Look for them in seed stores or in some vegetable stores. Remove the shells and put one peanut into each Jiffy pellet. When the roots fill the pellet, transfer it to a small flowerpot. The leaves are somewhat the same as those of the pea plant, and the yellow flowers look like small sweet peas. The bottom of the flower (ovary) pushes down into the ground and changes into a peanut there. Watch the leaves of the peanut plant fold together at night. They open again in the morning.

Seeds of apple, pear, peach, plum, and cherry need a cold treatment to get them to sprout. These seeds come from trees that grow where the winters are cold. The seeds drop to the ground in the winter and go through a cold period as they lie there. Then they are ready to sprout in the spring.

PEACH PLANT

To imitate this cycle, put the seeds in a plastic bag containing moist peat moss. Peat moss can be bought in the five-and-ten. Place the bag in the refrigerator, and leave it there for six to eight weeks. Then take the seeds out of the peat moss and plant them, one per Jiffy pellet. Treat and plant at least ten seeds because tree seeds do not sprout as readily as the seeds of other plants. Be sure to keep the pellet moist. When the roots fill the pellet, place the pellet in a pot containing soil.

In the winter put the pots outside in a window box. Protect them by putting dry peat moss between the pots and over the top of them. Bring the plants in when the buds begin to open.

Nuts, such as walnuts, filberts, almonds, and butternuts, need the same cold treatment as the fruit seeds.

If you look at the herb shelf in your grocery or supermarket, you will find many herb seeds. Try the mustard seed first. These seeds sprout quickly, and in a few days you can taste the pungent leaves.

MUSTARD SEEDLINGS

The seeds of coriander sprout within a week. In a short time, you will have a pretty plant with feathery leaves and pink flowers that look like Queen Anne's lace.

Try dill and fennel, both of which also have feathery leaves. They are difficult to transplant, so use the Jiffy pellets for these seeds.

Some health-food stores and many seed houses carry unroasted coffee beans, which grow into lovely small trees with dark-green, glossy leaves. Soak the seeds overnight, and plant one seed per Jiffy pellet. Move to a flowerpot when the roots fill the pellet.

DILL

SMALL COFFEE TREE

AVOCADO PIT

The biggest seed that comes into the house is the avocado. Remove the pit from the fruit, wash the flesh from the seed, and remove the brown papery coat. Stick three toothpicks around the middle of the seed evenly spaced. Then set the seed in a jar of water, *flat* end down, so that the bottom third of the pit is covered with water. Be sure to add water when needed to keep the bottom of the pit wet. Change the water once a week.

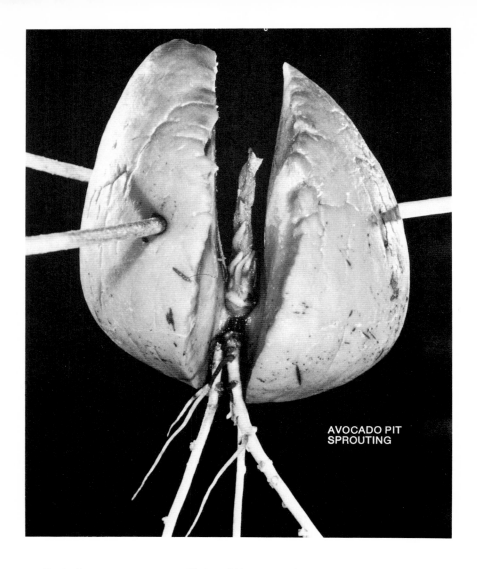

AVOCADO PIT
SPROUTING

It is best to use a tall jar like an olive jar, for although this seed takes weeks to get started, the roots grow fast and long once they start. Keep it in dim light while the roots are growing, and bring it out to the light when the stem starts to grow. You will be excited when you see the big seed split at the top to let out the stem and leaves.

AVOCADO PLANT

When it does, transfer the avocado to a pot one inch larger than the pit. Put some soil in the pot, place the pit on it, and fill in enough soil around it so that half the pit is exposed at the top. Place the pot where the plant will get bright light, and keep the soil moist. Let the plant grow naturally until it starts to branch. Then you can trim the side branches if they get too long.

BIRD AND GRASS SEED

BIRD AND GRASS SEED SPROUTING

Bird seed and grass seed are easy to get hold of and fun to watch growing. Sprinkle the seed over a wet sponge, and set the sponge in a saucer with water in it. Cover the sponge with a glass or plastic dish. When the seeds sprout, set the dish in a sunny window and take the glass cover off. Be sure to add water to the saucer to keep the sponge from drying out.

Every plant has a different way of growing. The best way to find out how beans, peas, melon, peanuts, and other common kitchen seeds grow is to plant them and see for yourself.

6

Plants Grow from Roots, Stems, and Leaves

Usually plants are thought to grow from seeds. But there are many other ways of raising them. They can grow from roots, from stems, and even from leaves.

If you want to try to grow a new plant from a root, you must find a root that has a lot of food stored in it. Sweet potatoes, carrots, beets, turnips, parsnips, and radishes all are such roots. They are good to eat because of the food stored in them. This same food helps a new plant grow.

You can make a beautiful vine grow out of a sweet potato, if it has not been dried in a kiln or treated with chemicals to keep it from growing. Go to a farmer's market or to a vegetable store, and ask for a sweet potato that shows some signs of life. If the buds look like little purple bumps, and if there are some roots hanging on, you have a good sweet potato to plant.

Set the sweet potato in a jar of water, so that only the narrow end is wet. If you don't have a jar that is the

SWEET POTATO

right size, stick toothpicks into the potato to support it at the mouth. Be sure to put the narrow pointed end into the water as the roots grow from it.

Now set the jar in a warm, dark place. Keep adding water as it is used up. The new roots will grow out first, and in about ten days you will see the stems starting. As soon as they appear, move the sweet potato into a sunny or brightly lighted window. The whole potato should become covered with stems and purple-veined leaves.

SWEET POTATO
SPROUTING

MORE MATURE SWEET-POTATO PLANT

You can let the vines trail over the sides of a container set in a hanging bracket, or you may prefer to tie the stems to cords and let them climb up the window.

The carrot root is easy to grow too. First take off the wilted leaves from the top of the carrot. Then cut off two inches of the carrot at the big end. Set the cut-off

CARROT

piece in a shallow bowl of water with pebbles or stones around it to hold it in place. If you cannot get your own stones, they can be bought at five-and-ten-cent stores. In a little while, new leaves will grow out of the top. They are thin and feathery, and they make a pretty table decoration.

BEET

PARSNIP

The other roots with stored food—beets, turnips, and parsnips—can be grown in exactly the same way.

A plain Irish potato is a stem. It is a funny kind of stem, because it grows under the ground. Like the sweet potato, it has food stored in it from which a new plant can grow.

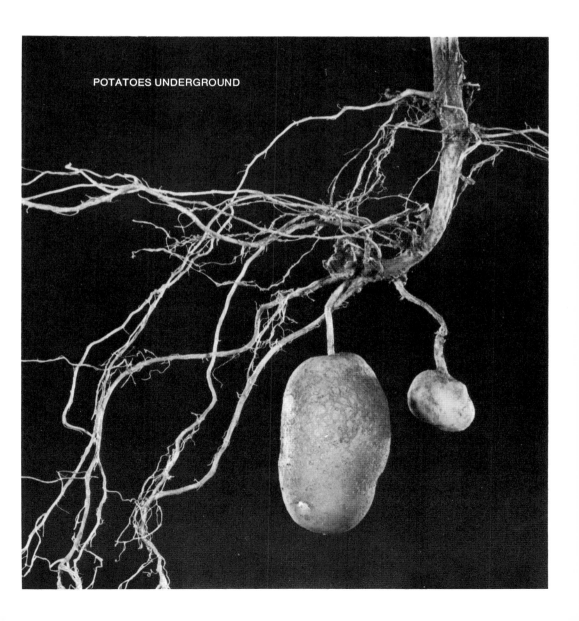

POTATOES UNDERGROUND

POTATO SPROUTING

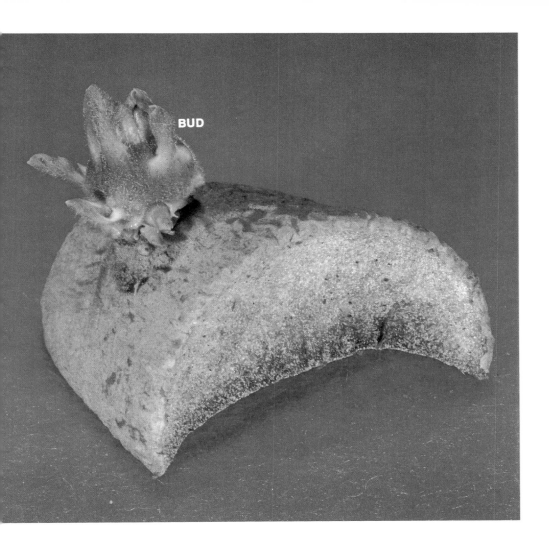

BUD

Put the potato in a jar of water, so that only the bottom stays wet. Roots will grow out from the lower end, and new stems and leaves will grow from the eyes, or little buds, which you can find on every potato. Try cutting off a piece of potato with two or three little buds on it. Let the cut-off end dry, and then plant it in a flowerpot. Put it about three inches below the surface of the soil. If you water it regularly, a potato plant will

POTATO PLANT

grow from this piece. Farmers plant their potato crops by using just such pieces of potato.

After the potato plant is about a foot tall, knock it out of the pot. Now you will see the potatoes that have been forming under the soil.

Another stem that has lots of stored food in it is the onion. An onion does not really look like a stem as it is very much shortened and flattened down, so that all its leaves are close together. We call such a stem a "bulb."

NEW POTATO
FORMING
UNDERGROUND

BUD ————

Cut down through the center of an onion, and you
will see the bud that can grow into a new plant.

Onions grow easily. In fact, you often find them growing in the bag without any help at all. If you want to
watch an onion grow, set it in a glass of water so that

LEAVES ——

ROOTS ——

only the bottom stays wet. New white roots will come out from the bottom of the bulb. The little bud inside then grows into long green leaves. The new young plant uses the food stored in the thick fleshy leaves of the bulb to get started. When your onion tops are about four inches

ONION,
GARLIC,
AND SHALLOT
BULBS

high, cut down through the middle of the bulb. You will see that the buds in the center have grown out into leaves. Garlic and shallot bulbs grow in the same way.

If you want pretty flowers to grow out of a bulb, try growing the paper-white narcissus. You can buy nar-

PAPER-WHITE
NARCISSUS

cissus bulbs at seed stores and at five-and-tens. You can grow these bulbs in water, holding them in place with pebbles.

First put a layer of pebbles in the bottom of a bowl. Then place the bulbs on them, adding more pebbles until just the ends of the bulbs are sticking out. Add enough water so that it will just touch the bottoms of the bulbs. Keep it at exactly that level. You will have to add a little water each day to do so. The bulbs use the water up, and it also evaporates in the air.

Place the bowl on a sunny windowsill. If you plant the bulbs late in the winter, they will bloom in about three weeks. If you start early in the fall, you will have to wait about two months for them to come into bloom. Narcissus bulbs bloom naturally in the spring. The nearer to this time they are planted in the house, the less time they take to grow.

Lots of plants can root from a piece of stem, or cutting. Cut off a piece of stem from a geranium plant. Make your cut just below a place where leaves come out of the stem. This place is called a "node." Trim off all but two or three leaves. Then plant the piece in moist sand, peat, or perlite in a container and slip a plastic bag over it.

After a few weeks you will see that your new plant is growing. Not every single plant you try will root in this way, but lots of plants will. Some, such as philodendron and ivy, will even take root in plain water. If a stem does

GERANIUM CUTTING

not seem to root easily, dip it first in a hormone powder called Rootone. This hormone makes it possible to root most cuttings.

When you see new leaves forming, you will know that the cutting has made new roots and so has become a

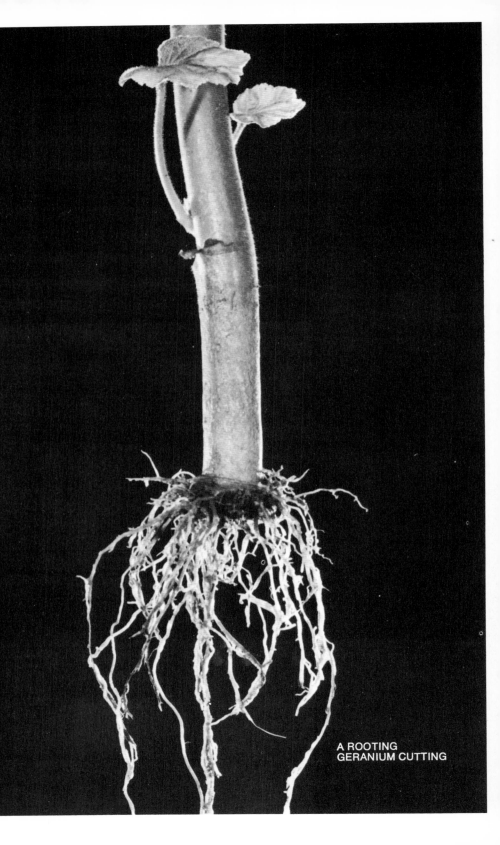

A ROOTING
GERANIUM CUTTING

whole new plant. Now is the time to move it into a pot containing soil.

So far you know how to start new plants from roots and stems. Starting new plants from leaves seems impossible. Yet you can do it with the leaves of some plants.

The crown of the pineapple fruit is a cluster of leaves, and it is easy to start a new plant from it. Simply cut off

PINEAPPLE CROWN

the crown where it meets the fruit. Leave no fruit on it. Then peel off the leaves at the bottom. From this core new roots will grow. Allow the bottom of the core to dry for a day. Then put the crown in a glass narrow enough to hold it up. The bottom of the core should be covered with water. When roots form, transfer the pineapple to a pot. The soil should come up to where the leaves start.

If you can get hold of a large, thick rex begonia leaf, make a cut at each large vein of the leaf and lay the leaf on damp vermiculite or perlite with the underside down. Put pebbles or stones on it to keep it flat.

REX-BEGONIA LEAF.

Now place a glass jar or a plastic box over it to keep it moist, and put it where it will get light. In a few weeks, tiny new plants will form where you made the cuts. When the new little plants are two to three inches tall, move them into separate small pots containing soil.

You can make lots of new plants from the leaves of the African violet. Take off a leaf with a little piece of

AFRICAN-VIOLET LEAF

AFRICAN-VIOLET LEAF
ROOTING

the stem attached and stand it up with the stem part buried in the damp vermiculite or perlite. Keep it covered with a glass jar. A tiny new plant will grow where the stem hits moist vermiculite or perlite.

Practically everybody owns a snake plant or at least

AFRICAN VIOLET

knows somebody who does. One of its long leaves can make more than a half-dozen new plants. To do so, cut up the leaf into pieces about two inches long, and place each piece halfway down into damp vermiculite or perlite. Cover all of the pieces with glass or plastic. New plants will form where the leaf hits the vermiculite or perlite.

If you become really interested in making new plants from cuttings or from leaves, get a small aquarium. Put a two-inch layer of perlite or vermiculite in it. Moisten

NEW PLANT

SNAKE PLANT

it. Then you can insert any cuttings or leaves you may want to root. Just keep the layer of perlite or vermiculite moist but not soaking wet. Cover the aquarium with a layer of Saran wrap to keep the moisture in.

You can experiment and find many other plants that will grow from a piece of stem or from a leaf.

If you have never grown anything before, start with the plants described in this book. The basic rules of planting are simple, and you can have great fun with the many seeds, roots, stems, and leaves that come into your kitchen and enable you to "play with plants."

Index

indicates illustration

Millicent E. Selsam's career has been closely connected with biology and botany. She majored in biology and was graduated *magna cum laude* with a B.A. degree from Brooklyn College. At Columbia she received her M.A. in the Department of Botany, and since then has passed all course requirements and a comprehensive examination for a Ph.D., also at Columbia. After teaching biology for ten years in the New York City high schools, she has devoted herself to writing science books for children.

Mrs. Selsam lives in New York City and spends her summers on Fire Island, New York.

Jerome Wexler was born in New York City, where he attended Pratt Institute. Later he studied at the University of Connecticut. His interest in photography started when he was in the ninth grade. After service in World War II, he worked for the State Department in Europe as a photographer. Returning to the United States, he specialized in photographing advanced farming techniques, and the pictures he made have been published throughout the world.

Now chief photographer for *Visual Teaching*, an audiovisual company specializing in slide sets and filmstrips for use in schools, Mr. Wexler lives in Wallingford, Connecticut.

5565

635
SEL

Selsam, Millicent E.

Play with plants

DATE			
NOV 2 3 '92			
DEC 1 9 '92			
NOV 1 4			
JAN 1 7 1995			

© THE BAKER & TAYLOR CO.